THE CONCISE HISTORIES OF **DEVON**

THE VIKINGS
AND DEVON

ACKNOWLEDGMENTS

I am very grateful to Julia Crick and John Allan who read an earlier draft of this manuscript, made helpful suggestions and corrected my errors. I am wholly responsible for what remains. My thanks go also to my wife, Anne, who volunteered to go to France while I wrote this and to Olivia who kept house.

THE CONCISE HISTORIES OF **DEVON**

THE VIKINGS
AND DEVON

DEREK GORE

First published in Great Britain by The Mint Press, 2001

© Derek Gore & The Mint Press 2001

The right of Derek Gore to be identified as author of this work has been asserted by him in accordance with the Copyright, Designs & Patents Act 1988.

ISBN 1-903356-11-3

Cataloguing in Publication Data
CIP record for this title is available from the British Library

The Mint Press
18 The Mint
Exeter, Devon
England EX4 3BL

Cover and text design by Delphine Jones

Main cover illustration, Helmeted head of a warrior found at Sigtuna, Sweden, courtsey of Antiquities and Topographical Archive, Stockholm.
Coin, Last small cross penny struck at Lydford (courtsey Exeter Museums Service).

Printed and bound in Great Britain
by Short Run Press Ltd, Exeter.

CONTENTS

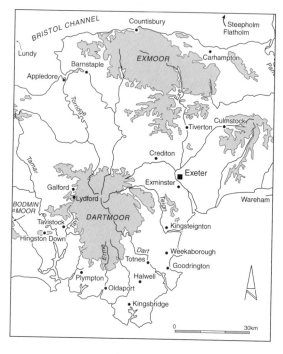

Viking Devon

THE
VIKINGS
AND
DEVON

Viking is a term which has been in use since the eleventh century for the Scandinavian sea-borne warriors who attacked western Europe from the later eighth century. Yet it was not a term they applied to themselves, preferring instead reference to a home region such as the Hörthaland(ers). Contemporary Christian writers called them pagans, heathens, northmen or gentiles. Skills in ship construction and handling reached a point in the eighth century where long voyages out of sight of land were possible. These skills had been honed in the Baltic, in the fiords and in the coastal waters off Norway and Denmark.

Viking warships were lightweight, flexible, oared vessels, with high prows and sterns. They did not require deep-water harbours, but could be dragged onto beaches or left at anchor. Built of oak and pine, with short lengths of strakes or sideboards fastened with metal rivets to a frame, the ships had a true keel with a mast step. They were constructed to ride over the waves rather than to cut through them. Manoeuvrability came from a choice of power - sail with a favourable wind, oars against the wind or in shallow waters, when the mast could be laid down lengthways. Warships varied in size up to about 30m long and 5m wide. The largest ships were capable of carrying around 100 men.

Our knowledge of Viking activities in western Europe stems from two sources of evidence - documentary and archaeological. The former consists largely of sets of annals, written by ecclesiastics invariably hostile to these pagan warriors. For Devon, one major source is the Anglo-Saxon Chronicle, written in old English and originally compiled in the southern English kingdom of Wessex about 893, towards the end of the reign of King Alfred and later continued in various monasteries in southern England. The account was written while the kingdom was under the threat of Viking attacks and not surprisingly it favours the West Saxons and Alfred's dynasty. An account of Alfred's life written by Asser, a Welsh bishop at court, also includes details of Viking activities in Devon. We are heavily reliant on sources such as these for dates, major events and names of leaders. The Vikings, on the other hand, produced no contemporary documentary record of their own. Their views were expressed only in later saga accounts of the late twelfth and later centuries, so far removed from the Viking Age that their value is difficult to assess.

We must be wary of the documentary evidence which has survived. We do not know how much has been lost, nor does the surviving record include every event which occurred. Also, all writers were selective. These writings were the focus of serious study from the sixteenth century onwards, from which time translations appeared. Their interpretation sparked lurid accounts of the Vikings. By the nineteenth century Scandinavians were being portrayed in art and in the pages of history books as lovers of gratuitous violence, who raped and pillaged their way through Christian Europe. Moreover, this simplistic view is still with us, although we are beginning to appreciate that situations could be much more complex, even on occasion subtle. In a period when most societies were in dread of all soldiers and armies, Viking war-bands were certainly feared and could be ruthless and destructive. However, as we shall see in Devon, their leaders were also capable of reading and acting upon political situations, of forming alliances, of stimulating economic activities and of working together for a common aim. Viking warriors could be heroic, honourable and loyal.

Archaeology, in contrast to the written material, may show us the shape, size and materials of contemporary structures and from small finds, something of the lives of the people who inhabited or used them. The interpretation of coins, place-names and stone sculptures adds to the picture by giving economic, settlement and art historical data. However, it should be stressed at the outset that the archaeological evidence for this period from Devon is sparse and uneven.

Written sources suggest that Norwegian Vikings were beginning to explore and raid through the Scottish islands into the Irish Sea from about 793. They may have penetrated into the English Channel and to the coast of Aquitaine. In so doing they are likely to have explored the Bristol Channel, the coasts of the South West and the Isles of Scilly - in this period a single large island with outliers. Danish Vikings were active in Frisia and along the Frankish Channel coast about a generation later.

It should be stressed, though, that we have no direct evidence of landings in Devon this early. Our written sources mention only landings in Scotland, Ireland, England and Aquitaine in these first two generations of exploration and raiding. However, there were certainly forms of contact between Scandinavia and western Europe, unmentioned in the written records, before this. Finds of Norwegian hone-stones, walrus ivory and reindeer antler in Europe and Anglo-Saxon and Frankish pennies in Denmark suggest pre-Viking Age contacts. Perhaps the Scandinavians were already familiar with parts of western Europe before exchanges turned to raiding.

DEVON
BEFORE THE
VIKINGS

Seaborne raiders would have found
Devon's two long sea coasts, totalling
together about 300 kms in length and
pierced by a number of navigable
estuaries and rivers interspersed,
especially on the south coast, with sandy
beaches, especially inviting. Vikings in the
initial stages of contact sought portable
wealth: silver, gold and slaves are
suggested by finds of hoards and by

written references. They returned home with their spoils at the end of each sailing season. However, from the middle of the ninth century Irish, English and Frankish sources suggest that some war-bands were staying over the winter at sites in western Europe, from which they continued to raid in the following season. It is also likely that by then some Scandinavian families had settled in the Scottish islands.

To understand the context of Viking activities within Devon, we need to know something of its background before the Viking Age. The word Devon in the forms *Defna* and *Defena* occurs for the first time in different versions of the Anglo-Saxon Chronicle for 823 or 825 as interpreted by modern scholars. The forms appear to be renderings into English of the Celtic word *Domnonia* or *Damnonia,* which occur in a text of the sixth-century writer Gildas and in a late seventh or very early eighth-century letter written by Abbot Aldhelm of Malmesbury to the British King Geraint in the South West. These continued the usage of the word *Dumnonii* for the people of the south-west peninsula preserved in inscriptions and medieval copies of itineraries from the Roman period. By the ninth century the words *Defna* or *Defena* seem to apply solely to the people of the area we would identify today as Devonshire, although that term does not occur until later, in 850 in the Chronicle, as *Defenascir.* The land boundaries of *Defenascir* were probably roughly those shown on modern maps, although there have been a number of minor alterations to both the western and eastern boundaries at different times.

When the Vikings first arrived off the Devon coast, the territory had only recently come under the control of the Anglo-Saxon kings of Wessex. Before that time the inhabitants were the descendants of the Britons, who had lived here in the pre-historic and Roman periods. When the peninsula ceased to be part of the Roman Empire in about AD 400, we can dimly perceive the growth of kingship and a British kingdom or kingdoms in the South West. Gildas mentions a king of Dumnonia called Constantine, who was the writer's contemporary, and, 150 years or so later, Abbot Aldhelm wrote to Geraint, King of Dumnonia. We do not know if these kings ruled over the whole of the South West, or whether their territories lay within that area. What Aldhelm does make plain is that Dumnonia was a Christian kingdom, with an organised Church, even though he disapproved of certain practices within the British Church. In a poem he described a journey he made eastwards from Cornwall (*Cornubia*) into Devon (*Dumnonia*).

To the east, the kingdom of the West Saxons, Wessex, had developed with its heartlands in Wiltshire and Hampshire. Its kings ruled over a mixed population of Britons, indigenous to the area, and

Germanic peoples, who had crossed to Britain from their homelands in north Germany from the fifth century onwards. The latter are popularly known as the Anglo-Saxons. The influence and authority of the kings of Wessex spread into surrounding areas. Not, as the Anglo-Saxon Chronicle would have us believe, solely by conquest but almost certainly by other mechanisms too. Germanic culture, especially language, was spread by the movement of families into new areas, by the acquisition of land and through the influence of the Church.

Wessex itself was only converted to Christianity from about 635 onwards. The distribution of pagan graves, typically accompanied with grave goods, in Wessex, which can be dated broadly from the fifth to the mid seventh centuries, shows a dense distribution in the heartlands. But there are far fewer burials known in Dorset and Somerset and none in Devon. This distribution implies that West Saxon material culture was not widely adopted in Dorset or Somerset before the mid seventh century at the earliest and not in Devon until somewhat later. Penselwood, on the boundary between Somerset, Dorset and Wiltshire, was perhaps an accepted boundary between the Britons to the west and the Anglo-Saxons to the east to the mid seventh century. Subsequent to this date, West Saxon kings are recorded granting lands to the British monastery at Glastonbury, Somerset and by 722 the West Saxon King Ine had built a fortification at Taunton.

The Life of St Boniface, missionary to the Saxons east of the Rhine, mentions his education at a monastery in Exeter about 690. Much later tradition suggests he was born near Crediton. Boniface's birth name was Wynfrith and the abbot of his monastery was Wulfheard - both Anglo-Saxon names. This evidence has been used to suggest that before 700 the Exe Valley and Exeter were under the control of the West Saxon kings, but this is unlikely. It is much more likely that there was contact between the two areas for a considerable time before the West Saxon kings were acknowledged as rulers in Devon. The earliest charters issued by kings of Wessex confirming transfer of estates in Devon cluster along the eastern border at Culmstock, Culm Davey and Uplyme with two exceptions only - a grant of land in the valley of the Torridge, north Devon, of 729 and a grant of 739 of an estate at Crediton to Bishop Forthere of Sherborne. Assuming all these charters are genuine they suggest that West Saxon kings were not exercising power in Devon before some decades into the eighth century.

In 802 Egbert succeeded to the throne of Wessex after a period of exile in Francia. In the course of a long reign, he enlarged the kingdom and founded a new, stable dynasty. The succession was organised, as it had not been previously, so that a son or a brother followed the previous king onto the throne. By Egbert's reign, Vikings, as we have seen, were already active around the English coasts. Their presence may have been one factor which helped to stabilise the West Saxon succession.

Egbert was probably responsible for consolidating the West Saxon hold on Devon. He extended his control over much of the area south of the Thames, largely at the expense of his rivals, the kings of Mercia, whose power lay in the Midlands, but who in the 8th and early 9th centuries had exercised power over Kent and other eastern territories. During the course of the ninth century Mercia became increasingly dependent upon

Wessex. In 815 the Chronicle reported Egbert ravaging in Cornwall from east to west, that is presumably along the spine of the territory perhaps along the line of the modern A30 road. Ten years later the Britons engaged the men of Devon at *Gafolford*, probably Galford, near Lydford in west Devon. The mention of the men of Devon again suggests that by now the bulk of Devon was fully part of Wessex but that the Britons of Cornwall had not been cowed by the ravaging ten years previously. Additionally, the Britons seem to have taken the fight into Devon, east of the Tamar, into an area between Bodmin Moor and Dartmoor, which may still have been in dispute. Egbert himself may have been engaged against the Britons of the

South West in the summer of 825, if the unusual dating in a forged Winchester charter is reliable. It recorded his presence on 19 August 825 at *Criodantreow*, a place not identified, when the king was moving his army against the Britons.

The river Tamar, for much of its length, forms a linguistic boundary between Celtic place-names to the west and predominantly Anglo-Saxon or Old English names to the east. Celtic names of farmsteads and settlements were probably replaced with Old English names as West Saxon influence grew in Devon. In addition newly-founded settlements would also have been named in Old English. By contrast, in Cornwall there are very few Old English names except in a narrow band close to the Tamar valley. Oliver Padel has suggested that wholesale name changes occurred because place-names were not yet in written form at the time when the West Saxons took control of Devon, whereas Anglo-Saxon control of Cornwall was achieved only after the bulk of the settlement names had already been written down. The eighth century is the likeliest period for the name changes in Devon. The pattern of place-names on modern maps therefore reflects the contrasting history of the two territories.

THE
VIKINGS
ARRIVE

In the reign of Egbert's predecessor, Beorhtric, between 789 and 802, the Chronicle recounts that three Viking ships landed in his kingdom. According to the Chronicle this was the first landing by the Northmen on English soil and if true this event should pre-date the famous attack on the monastery at Lindisfarne on Holy Island off the Northumbrian coast in 793 and moreover be the first record of a landing anywhere in the British Isles. Two versions of the Chronicle assert that these were Northmen from Hörthaland, west Norway, and if so one view would see this event as an extension of the Viking exploration of the Irish Sea. Other sources suggest that the landing was at Portland Bill, on the Dorset coast and that the local reeve, or royal official, from nearby Dorchester went to escort the arrivals to the town, as the law required for merchants arriving on the boundary of the kingdom. The reeve, with few followers, was promptly killed. This episode is open to different interpretations. This might have been a raiding-army intent on loot or a small

party of traders who took fright or
offence at the attitude of the reeve. It
may also remind us that the line between
trading and raiding might have been
blurred. It was another 40 years before
the next recorded landing in Wessex.

In 836 the Chronicle recorded a
battle at Carhampton, just over the
Devon border on the north Somerset
coast. Thirty-five ships (or 25 as reported
in three versions of the Chronicle)
landed in an area that was to witness a
number of Viking attacks over the next
200 years. Care is needed over the size of
fleets mentioned in the Chronicle.
Figures suggest an army of between 1000
and 3000 men, but the annalist may have
exaggerated the number of ships to

make Egbert's eventual defeat appear more heroic. Egbert fought them but after great slaughter the Vikings had possession of the battlefield, that is they were not driven away by the Anglo-Saxons. The Vikings probably targeted Carhampton for two reasons. The bay between Minehead and Watchet had suitable beaches for landing and in particular the beach below Carhampton itself, at Blue Anchor, still popular with holidaymakers, would have been inviting to the fleet.

Secondly, Carhampton was almost certainly the centre of a royal estate. It was mentioned in Alfred's will, left on his death in 899 to his son and successor Edward the Elder. Recent field work in the area has revealed high status activity and pottery from the fifth and sixth centuries, suggesting tentatively that the site might have been a British estate centre before it was acquired by the West Saxons. Viking leaders chose royal and ecclesiastical centres for their attacks, presumably with the expectation of acquiring portable wealth at such places, because they were populous centres and they were likely to be able to feed their troops there. The north Somerset coast between Porlock and the Quantocks is rich farming country and a number of Anglo-Saxon royal estates were situated there. This is a pattern of Viking activity which we should note. In particular there are two important considerations, which may help us to understand Viking tactics in Devon. This attack on Carhampton shows that Viking leaders acquired information about landing places and potential targets, as well as most probably tides, currents and likely opposition. These raids were not as opportunistic as is sometimes suggested. Also it is extremely unlikely that this attack is as isolated as a reading of the Chronicle suggests. Our written sources were almost certainly only recording major events, where the king or royal officials were involved. What is missing from the record are more minor events in between.

Two years later the Chronicle reported a further development. The

Britons of Cornwall formed an alliance
with a Viking army and attacked Wessex.
How this agreement was forged is open
to speculation, but it seems likely that the
Cornish were keen to gain strong allies
against their traditional enemies. The
Chronicle notes the Viking army came to
Cornwall, so whether the agreement was
planned or made on the spur of the
moment we do not know. It does,
however, illustrate the point that Viking
leaders were prepared to reach
agreements against an enemy, that they
developed political aims or at least that
they were prepared this early to act as
mercenaries. Were they promised
portable wealth or land for settlement by
the Cornish? Was the agreement

negotiated by a Cornish king? In 838 Egbert defeated a combined army of Cornish and Vikings at Hingston Down near Callington, just west of the Tamar and there, as the Chronicle reported, he put the combined army to flight.

In the reign of Aethelwulf, Egbert's son, from 839 to 858 Wessex continued to be attacked by Viking fleets. In 843 Carhampton was again targeted by a Viking raiding-army and Aethelwulf was defeated there, but five years later local levies inflicted a defeat on a Viking force at the mouth of the river Parret. In 850 the Devon levies led by their ealdorman, Ceorl, heavily defeated a Viking army at a place called *Wicganbeorg*, the location of which is uncertain, though one possibility among several is Weekaborough, now a small hamlet inland from Torquay, which would suggest a landing in Torbay.

ALFRED
AND THE
VIKINGS

I n 865 a Viking army assembled in the kingdom of East Anglia. The Chronicle calls it a '*micel here*', that is 'great army', and it and other sources suggest that it was led by the brothers Ivarr and Halfdan. It was joined in 871 by a second army termed by the Chronicle 'the Summer army' and led by Guthrum. It is significant that about this time our sources do begin to name Viking leaders and to style them on occasion 'kings'. These armies were composed of separate war-bands, whose warriors were prepared to accept overall direction by high status leaders. These armies seem to be larger than, or at least better organised than, those operating previously in England and more importantly their aims were different. Conquest of kingdoms was now the aim with the further goals of control and settlement of their lands. In all of these the armies were very successful. Between 866 and 874 they seized three of the four English kingdoms. In the process the kings of Northumbria and East Anglia were killed and the king of Mercia fled abroad. In 875 an army led by Guthrum, which had over-wintered in Cambridge, managed to evade the West Saxon army, crossed Wessex and seized Wareham in Dorset. In conjunction, a Viking fleet sailed into the great natural harbour at Poole, three kilometres down the river Frome from Wareham.

Alfred, by now king of Wessex, brought an army to Wareham, where the Vikings over-wintered. Alfred seems to have been content to sit and wait, making no attempt to storm the site. We do not know the size of either army, but Viking forces were always difficult to defeat when occupying strongholds. Wareham was well protected, by the rivers Frome to the south and Piddle to the north and by marshland to the east. If Wareham was already protected by earthwork defences this would have been an added attraction.

In 876 Alfred managed to reach agreement with his enemy that they would leave Wessex. The Viking leaders offered hostages as surety and swore oaths on a ring sacred to them to leave. However, the army, already mounted as the Chronicle stresses, moved swiftly to Exeter. Fleet and army acted once again in concert, since at about the same time the fleet appears to have sailed from Poole with Exeter as its goal. Exeter was a good choice, accessible from the sea and fortified. The Chronicle makes it clear that Guthrum's force knew where it was going before it set out from Wareham. Alfred pursued the force, but was unable to catch it before it reached Exeter. The movements of the Viking armies in this period demonstrate the intelligence available to them and their knowledge of sites and of the coastline. Did they make for Exeter because they believed Devon was not firmly part of Alfred's kingdom? Was there some expectation of British support?

On this occasion, however, the Vikings were defeated by the weather. Off Swanage the fleet lost 120 ships in a storm and, whether we believe the exact figure or not, this must have been a severe blow to the operation. Exeter still had its Roman walls, some two thirds of which survive today, though altered and repaired. The city wall was over two kilometres long enclosing an area of 37 hectares and it is this size which poses a problem for historical analysis.

The Chronicle states that once the Vikings had occupied Exeter Alfred could not get at them. As at Wareham, a Viking army behind defences was dangerous and difficult to defeat. However, it is hard to believe that the Vikings had sufficient forces to man the Exeter defences adequately. Even if we add the depleted ships' crews overwintering within the defences, it is unlikely that the Scandinavians could have held the whole circuit of the Roman walls against an enemy. One solution could be that they occupied only one corner of the defences - perhaps the southern end nearest the river and presumably with their ships sheltering beneath them. This would have required them to construct some form of temporary defence across part of the city, something of which they were perfectly capable. At Reading in 870-1 and again at Repton in 873-4 Viking armies had built earthwork defences to protect themselves over the winter.

Once again, in 877, Alfred was offered hostages and great oaths were sworn by the Vikings to ensure that they would leave his kingdom and they departed at harvest-time into Mercia to the ex-Roman city of Gloucester. Again the attractions must have been the Roman defences and Gloucester's access to the sea via the river Severn and the

Bristol Channel. Gloucester lay only some 25 kilometres beyond the West Saxon northern border and, with hindsight, was carefully chosen by the Viking leadership. In view of future events it seems likely that the autumn and winter in Gloucester were spent developing and co-ordinating plans.

Alfred probably celebrated Christmas at the royal vill at Chippenham, the centre of an important royal estate. The Viking army moved early in January and seized Chippenham and occupied Wessex. The move was unusual in early medieval warfare, since it was very rare for armies to attempt operations in the winter. Alfred was obviously taken by surprise and unprepared and had to flee with a small force. Some West Saxons submitted; others fled. Guthrum and the other Viking leaders must have assumed at this point, given the pattern of the previous ten years, that the last of the English kingdoms, Wessex, was now in their hands.

The Chronicle, Bishop Asser and a later tenth-century writer, Aethelweard, all recount different versions of a second action by Vikings at this time. A brother of Ivarr and Halfdan, whom a much later source named as `Ubbe', moved in the winter of 877-8 from raiding in Dyfed, south-west Wales, to the north Devon coast with a fleet of 23 ships. It is difficult to believe that these two Viking forces were acting entirely independently of each other. Both moved in the winter and both attacked Wessex. The most likely explanation is that these were co-ordinated moves against Alfred perhaps even with the specific intention of capturing or killing him. It is interesting that a landing was made on the north Devon coast, which was some distance from the main area of action.

However, Asser and Aethelweard assert that the Viking army's first objective was to deal with a Devon force, Aethelweard says led by Ealdorman Odda, which was within a fortification at *arx Cynuit*. Asser further explains that *Cynuit* was a stronghold, unprepared except for ramparts constructed in the Celtic fashion, presumably earthworks,

yet with strong natural defences on every
side except from the east. The site was so
strongly positioned that the Vikings laid
siege to it, believing that lack of food and
water would soon starve the defenders
out. The besiegers were therefore taken
by surprise when the Saxons emerged out
of the stronghold at dawn and
overwhelmed them, killing the afore-
mentioned Ubbe with 800 of his men
(Asser says 1200) and 40 men of his
personal retinue. Their raven banner was
captured and few men escaped back to
their ships. Curiously Aethelweard asserts
that the Vikings won, even though their
leader was killed.

Asser makes clear that he had seen
the site at *Cynuit* and his description of it

therefore carries weight. Appledore, Bideford, Cannington and Countisbury have all been advanced. Local antiquaries from the seventeenth century onwards attempted to identify the site of the battle and of Ubbe's burial mound. Both Kenwith Castle at Abbotsham near Bideford and a mound near Appledore, which had disappeared into the sea, have had their advocates but these may be dismissed as without substance.

All sources are clear that the events took place in Devonshire, which would seem to exclude Cannington, Somerset, which appeared on early ordnance survey maps as the site of the battle. The name Cannington, which some took to be derived from *Cynuit*, is *Cantactune* in its earliest form in King Alfred's will, that is Quantock Town, the settlement at the approach to the Quantock Hills. In any case this interpretation was based on the finds of human bones, taken to be evidence of a battle close to a known Iron Age hillfort. Excavation has shown that the remains are from a late Roman and early medieval cemetery, which had ceased to be used by the ninth century.

The promontory fort on Wind Hill, Countisbury, rising to 240m above Lynmouth fits Asser's description best. It is a roughly triangular-shaped fort of about 50 hectares with precipitous slopes on all but its eastern side. Here, a 400 metre length of imposing rampart still survives with the top of the rampart some

8 metres vertical above the bottom of the ditch, effectively cutting off the approach from the east, as Asser says. Can we explain the presence of the king's thegns or nobles and their followers in this area as described in Asser's account? The hillfort lies above the mouth of the east and west Lyn rivers, one of the few landing places on this stretch of coast. Had the thegns gathered in the ancient earthwork in expectation of an attack or did the settlers of the area seek refuge in it or is it possible that there was a permanent settlement within the hillfort?

Different interpretations have been offered for the derivation of the name. In Domesday Book Countisbury is entered as

Contesberia, where the *beria* element comes from Anglo-Saxon *burh* or fortification. It has been argued that *contes* was a form of Welsh *cunet*, a hill or that it was a British river-name as in *Cunetio*, that is the River Kennet, Wiltshire, derived out of the Latin *Cynuit*. Oliver Padel has suggested that a Brittonic personal name is also possible in view of the English genitival form, but that whichever interpretation is favoured, there is no philological objection to the identification. The derivation of the name is therefore relatively unimportant compared with the identification of the site and on this modern scholars agree that *arx Cynuit* is most plausibly identified with Countisbury.

Despite the defeat of the Viking army at *Cynuit,* the position of Wessex and its king appeared to be desperate in the early months of 878. Alfred eventually found refuge at Athelney in the Somerset Levels, from where he organised resistance. His position was perhaps not as weak as our sources suggest. He was able by May 878 to gather an army and engage the enemy at Edington in Wiltshire. Here on the battlefield and in the aftermath the Saxons gained a complete victory and the surrender of the Viking leaders. As a result Guthrum and the other leaders took their war-bands into Mercia and East Anglia, where they settled those lands.

According to the sources Wessex was largely free from Viking attacks for the next fourteen years, a period of weak rule in Francia, which led the Danes to target that country. Alfred took the opportunity to introduce reforms and develop policies. Both Scandinavians and English had appreciated the value of fortifications over the previous twenty years. The Mercian kings of the mid-to-late eighth century had used the land tax system to raise labour to repair and build fortifications. Charter evidence suggests that at least since the reign of Alfred's father Aethelwulf in the 840s the West Saxon kings had done the same. As we have seen there were already fortified places in Wessex. Alfred now extended and developed the system. Copies of documents survive, known collectively to

modern scholars as the Burghal Hidage.
This is an early tenth-century list of *burhs*
or fortified places and the arrangements
made to build, repair and garrison them.
Substantially it refers to the situation in
Alfred's reign.

A number of hides or tax units was
attached to each site and one man was
provided for service from each hide. The
list gives the number of men required to
garrison each site. A formula at the end
of one document explains that four men
were needed to guard one pole, that is 16
feet 6 inches or 5.03 metres, of rampart.
Four places are listed in Devon - Exeter,
Halwell in the South Hams, Lydford in
west Devon and Pilton by Barnstaple. The
geographical spread, covering all parts of

the shire was deliberate. The aim was to provide safe refuges in all parts of the kingdom. These sites would then be denied to the enemy and would hamper their movements. Former Roman sites with existing defences such as Exeter, former Iron Age sites like Halwell or Pilton, and naturally defensible sites such as Lydford were typical of those chosen. Once the threat of Viking attacks receded it was probably envisaged that some forts would be abandoned. Others were already settlements or would attract settlement and become permanent.

Excavations at Lydford burh have shown that earthwork defences were built around a wedge-shaped promontory of 8 hectares. The find of a single sherd of fifth or sixth-century pottery hints at occupation before the late ninth century. The rampart, 12 metres across and still standing in places to a vertical height of 3 metres, was constructed of turf with alternate layers of saplings and some larger timber strapping. Vertical post-holes within the body of the rampart suggest supports for fighting platforms or towers. Internal planning, which may not be contemporary with rampart construction, included a spinal street with side streets. Property boundaries and traces of timber buildings of Anglo-Saxon date were revealed. The excavations at Lydford, therefore, provide some details of the features of one Devon burh which may be indicative of others.

The West Saxon kings provided the opportunity for towns to develop in Devon. Halwell and Pilton were probably abandoned during Edward's reign but Totnes, Kingsbridge, Plympton and Barnstaple are likely tenth-century urban centres. The attraction of fortifications for royal, ecclesiastical and economic functions in periods of uncertainty is obvious. Exeter, for example, was the site of a mint in the last few years of Alfred's reign. This has suggested to Maddicott a growth of trade into and out of Exeter from the 890s and consequent access to silver for minting purposes. This was perhaps the beginning of the importance of trade with Ireland and northern France through Devon ports.

Devon was already divided into hides for tax purposes so the numbers which could be assigned to these four places were already known. Exeter, for example, was assigned 734 hides giving a defensive circuit of 923 metres, less than half its true length of 2354 metres. There is a similar discrepancy in the assignment for Lydford. Apparent anomalies occur elsewhere in the list too. Nicholas Brooks has pointed out that the likeliest explanation is that there were insufficient hidage units to assign and therefore some sites had to be content with smaller garrisons. The number of hides for Devon and Cornwall in Domesday Book is very close to the total for all four burhs. He suggests that labour was raised from the Cornish hides for the west Devon burhs. It is probably significant that there were no burhs listed for Cornwall. Perhaps the West Saxon kings did not trust the Britons of Cornwall or they lacked full control there.

Wessex was attacked by Viking armies leaving Francia from 892. They were active in England for the next four years operating mainly from bases in Essex. Their lack of success, mentioned in the Chronicle under 896, must in part have been due to the building of *burhs*. This was well-illustrated by events in Devon in 893 when fleets from Viking-held Northumbria and East Anglia laid siege to a fort on the north Devon coast - perhaps Pilton - and besieged Exeter.

Neither was reported as taken and Alfred brought an army west to relieve Exeter. The Viking fleet departed at his approach.

Alfred died in October 899 and made careful provision for the defence of Devon in his will. His son and successor Edward the Elder received an estate at Hartland as well as other lands in north Cornwall and Somerset. The intention was surely that Edward, with these holdings, would be helped to defend the Bristol Channel coast. Alfred's second son, Aethelweard, was left a string of estates in the southern half of the shire, including Tiverton, Exminster, Lustleigh and Lifton. Again these were part of a pattern in which Aethelweard inherited lands close to the south coast of Wessex, presumably in the expectation that these landholdings would help him to protect that boundary and assist his brother in defending the kingdom.

LATER VIKING ACTIVITIES

Edward took further steps to protect Devon. At the beginning of his reign he exchanged the minster and estate at Plympton, which was owned by the bishopric of Sherborne, for three vills in Somerset. Fleming has shown that this was part of a process which saw the Crown or its secular officials acquire a number of manors from the Tamar to the Dart between then and the Norman

Conquest. She believes that these lands were used to control the rivers of the South Hams to prevent incursions by seaborne raiders. In 917 the Chronicle reported that Edward had set up positions from which the Bristol Channel coast between Cornwall and Avonmouth could be guarded against a Viking fleet which had arrived in those waters from Brittany.

No attacks on Devon were reported during Edward's reign or for more than fifty years after. The tenth century marked a lull in Viking activity in most of Europe. Scandinavian settlers north of the Thames were gradually converted to Christianity and an Anglo-Scandinavian society emerged from a mingling of cultures. Edward's son, Athelstan, was active in Devon too, if the early twelfth-century writer William of Malmesbury is accurate. He reported that Athelstan fortified Exeter with walls and towers. A recent detailed survey of the walls has revealed late Saxon repairs and the addition of a parapet close to the north corner of the defences in Northernhay Gardens, though these cannot of course be attributed specifically to Athelstan. An excavation in 1990 at Lower Coombe Street inside the defences on the south-east side revealed that a minor lane laid out in the late ninth century ran along the inside of the wall, presumably to service the defences. However, the area was sparsely populated before the thirteenth century when tenements were laid out. Prior to that this area was cultivated and traces of ridge and furrow ploughing of the eleventh century were encountered. Other peripheral sites in the south-western half of the walled area have shown an absence of late Saxon occupation.

Excavations in the central part of the town, especially the area between the later cathedral and the north-western defences, have shown considerable activity in the tenth and eleventh centuries. Under Cathedral Close a cemetery, dating possibly from the seventh century and almost certainly aligned to a church, perhaps St Boniface's monastic church, has been revealed. This was followed by a later cemetery and substantial minster church, which tradition suggests was founded by Athelstan. Allan, Higham and Henderson have drawn attention to areas of regular street layout and tenement blocks between Paul Street and High Street, where rubbish pits have yielded evidence of occupation and craftworking, and between Catherine Street and High Street as well as along Fore Street. This was probably one planning episode of the late tenth century and shows that the central part of the town was occupied in the late Saxon period.

Athelstan was certainly active about this time in Devon. He issued a charter from the town, described therein as a royal citadel, in 928 and apart from this stay at Exeter he held councils at Lifton in 931 and at Exeter again about 935. In addition William of Malmesbury reported, obscurely, that Athelstan attacked the Britons and drove them out of Exeter, which they had occupied jointly with the English and fixed the boundary of their province at the Tamar. The latter comments are difficult to interpret but generally they illustrate the problems English kings faced in the South West and they appear to show that friction still existed between the different elements of the population. William speaks of the wealth of the town, the abundance of manufactured goods found there and the number of outsiders crowding its streets. This is supported by the quantity of Saxo-Norman imported pottery, mostly from northern France, recovered as well as the finds of a gold ring and a copper alloy strap end from excavations in Cathedral Close which also hint at wealthy citizens.

Viking raids and campaigns against England began again in 980 in the reign of Aethelred II. The first attacks on the South West were probably by Irish Norse, but within a short time prominent Danish and Norwegian leaders were leading armies to England composed of Vikings from Denmark, Norway and Sweden. The kingdom of England, created by the efforts of West Saxon

kings, was targeted. Other areas of
Europe were too well defended to entice
attack. The tribute paid to these armies
and their raiding successes encouraged
them to return and awoke political
ambitions. From 994 Svein, the king of
Denmark, led armies in England in
person and Olaf Tryggvason, later briefly
king of Norway, was another leader.

The monastery at Padstow on the
river Camel was sacked in 981 and in the
same year the Devon coast was attacked.
Between 995 and 997 a great fleet was
active around Devon, attacking first the
Bristol Channel coasts and then
returning around Land's End to sail up
the Tamar and Tavy to Tavistock, where
they attacked the abbey and on to the

burh at Lydford, which apparently held
out against them. However the Chronicle
reports that they brought immense booty
back to their ships. It is possible that
Svein led these attacks, before returning
to Denmark. The Danish fleet returned
from Normandy in 1001 and sailed into
the Teign, where the royal centre at
Kingsteignton was burnt together with
other residences. They moved on into
the Exe, made a determined attack on
Exeter, which was repulsed and then
reached Pinhoe, where two of the king's
reeves opposed them with an army, but
were defeated. They went on to burn
Pinhoe, Clyst and other manors and
escaped with much booty.

Exeter, however, was taken two years

later, when an army led by Svein attacked the town. The Chronicle reported that the town fell because of the treachery of a 'French', that is a Norman, reeve, Hugh, who had been appointed by Queen Emma, herself a Norman. The Chronicler may here be revealing his bias and when he goes on to report the wholesale destruction of the borough there may be an element of exaggeration.

Certainly by now the town was worth plundering. Metcalf has shown that as the volume of coins minted in Chester declined fairly rapidly, from about 973, the production from south-western mints increased. He believes that there was a change in the direction of trade in the

Irish Sea at about this time, with coins
minted at Barnstaple, Lydford and
Exeter beginning to appear in Ireland.
Exeter in particular was outminting
Chester by about 980 and was ranked
fifth in terms of mint output in England
in Aethelred's reign. Maddicott, however,
sees the origins of the Irish trade with the
South West one hundred years earlier
and suggests that Exeter may have
become the centre for the processing
and export of Dartmoor tin in this
period.

One way in which Aethelred
attempted to counteract the
Scandinavian menace was to strengthen
the *burhs* and order the construction of
others. In Devon there are two possible

examples of work of this period. Firstly, the wall of granite blocks inserted into the front of the north-eastern defences at Lydford most likely dates from the reign of Aethelred. The Alfredian *burhs* at Cricklade and Wareham were similarly strengthened. Secondly, Rainbird has argued recently that the site at Oldaport, near Modbury may be an unfinished Aethelredan burh, founded to provide extra defence for the south Devon estuaries in addition to Kingsbridge, Totnes and Plympton. Oldaport may be compared to Cadbury Castle, near Yeovil in Somerset, where excavation has shown that this Iron Age hillfort was refurbished with a stone wall inserted into the top of its inner earthen rampart early in the eleventh century. This was a new *burh*, occupied for about ten years between 1010 and 1020, and the site of a mint transferred to it from nearby Ilchester.

Svein was briefly king of England in 1013/4, when Aethelred fled to Normandy, and his son Knut took the throne from 1016. With a Scandinavian king on the throne, England was safe from further Viking attack, a situation which continued until the death of Edward the Confessor, in January 1066. Events in this year led to the Norman Conquest. Edward's successor, Harold II, of the Godwin family, was half Danish through his mother Gytha. He had extensive landholdings in Devon and after his defeat and death at Hastings in October 1066 at the hands of another leader of Scandinavian descent, William, Duke of Normandy, Harold's mother and probably some of his sons held Exeter against the new king. The situation caused William to lead an army into the South West in the winter of 1068. He laid siege to Exeter, which held out against him for eighteen days. Gytha escaped, perhaps down the Exe, and took refuge on Flatholm Island in the Bristol Channel.

Harold's sons obtained help from the king of Dublin, who allowed them to recruit Hiberno-Norse mercenaries and a fleet, with which they returned into the Bristol Channel in the summer of 1068.

An attack on Bristol failed and after a successful action further down the coast they returned to Dublin with booty. The following year they appeared again in the South West with a larger fleet and perhaps sailed into the Exe, but lacking support may have attacked the south Devon coast. A note in the Exeter Domesday Book recorded nine manors laid waste by the Irish between the Erme and the Kingsbridge estuary and it is possible that this happened now. Another intriguing possibility is that an armlet of twisted gold wires with a facetted rectangular knob found on Goodrington beach in 1978 might have been dropped by one of these raiders. The closest parallels are from

Scandinavia, especially a hoard from the island of Gotland in the Baltic of mid eleventh-century date. However, it is impossible to prove the connection. With the failure of the Hiberno-Norse expedition of 1069, led by Harold's sons, the Viking Age in Devon ended.

Intermittent Scandinavian activities on the coasts of Devon over a 250 year period do not appear to have resulted in permanent occupation or settlement. The distribution of Scandinavian place-name elements in South Wales from Cardiff westwards and especially in Pembroke suggests some settlement there. The islands in the Channel, Steepholm, Flatholm and Lundy, together with many of the islands closer to the Welsh coast, have Scandinavian names but such elements are lacking from Devon names. The usual interpretation is that islands received names as navigational points or bases. Lundy is probably Old Norse *lund* - puffin, with *ey* - island hence puffin island. It is mentioned in the Orkneyinga Saga or The History of the Earls of Orkney, which was written in Iceland about 1200. The work gives written form to oral tradition and was not necessarily giving historical facts, but it does show the use of the island as a stronghold in the Viking Age. On one occasion a Welsh chief fled to a fort on Lundy, which was besieged unsuccessfully by Scandinavians and on another a Viking leader took refuge with the same Welsh chief on Lundy.

Lundy lies some 20 kilometres north of Hartland Point in the approaches to the Bristol Channel. It is a substantial granite Tor, 5 kilometres long and rising to 123 metres, with a sheltered landing beach at its south-east point. Viking fleets were active in the Bristol Channel on different occasions through the period, as we have seen, so it is no surprise that they named and made use of the island. There is some support for Viking use of the island in the ninth century. Gardner and Ternstrom have examined the evidence for the discovery in 1856 of human remains on the edge of the modern settlement at the south end of the island. The find of a 'giant's grave' was reported close to an area which more recent archaeological work has demonstrated was the site of a fifteenth to seventeenth-century cemetery and middens. Two blue glass beads and two fragments of gilt bronze were later reported from the burial and deposited in Bristol Museum. Recent examination of these suggests that the beads are Hiberno-Norse types of ninth-century date and the metal fragments may be part of a Scandinavian oval brooch. Pairs of oval brooches were worn high on the breast by Norse women, pinned to the straps of an apron dress and sometimes with a necklace slung between them. There is a possibility therefore that the

1856 diggers uncovered a Viking burial. The beads and brooch would however suggest a female burial, so perhaps the modern burials had disturbed much earlier interments.

The authors of the Devon place-name volumes found very few names with Scandinavian elements and more research by Wakelin on Cornwall and the South West reached the same conclusion. There is a very small cluster of names in the South Hams, between the rivers Avon and Dart. These are three hybrid names, with the common Anglo-Saxon *tun* ending, meaning a settlement prefixed by a possible Scandinavian personal name. They are Grimston, Gripstone and Oldstone made up respectively from the names *Grimr*, *Gripr* and *Ulfr*. The fact that they do lie in a close cluster is interesting, but we should not necessarily interpret them as evidence for Scandinavian settlers. Domesday Book shows how popular Scandinavian personal names became in England. Also *tun* names continued to be formed up to and after the Norman Conquest, so these names may be late formations. Grimston is recorded in Domesday as *Grismetone*, but Oldstone is first recorded as *Olvyston* only in 1330 and Gripstone as *Cribeston* or *Grypeston* in 1244. The presence of a tiny number of similar names just over the border in east Cornwall hardly strengthens the case for settlement by Scandinavians in the

Viking Age. One faint possibility remains however, that these were formed in the reigns of Knut or his sons.

The dedication of a church on Fore Street to Saints Olave, Mary and Thomas the Apostle by 1063 might be thought to indicate Scandinavians living by then in Exeter. Olafr Helgi was the king of Norway who completed the conversion of the Norwegians to Christianity, using rather brutal methods, before his death in battle in 1030. Within five years he was declared a saint and martyr and his cult spread quickly throughout Scandinavia and Europe. In England, he was especially popular in urban churches such as Chester, York, Norwich and London, all of which might be said from other evidence to have had citizens of Scandinavian descent. However churches at Chichester, Bradford on Avon and Poughill in north-east Cornwall were also dedicated to Olave without these settlements having any obvious direct Scandinavian connections. At Exeter, however, St Olave's was granted land by Gytha, Harold's Danish mother, between 1057 and 1065. Was she the foundress? It should be noted that King Edward the Confessor also gave a grant to the church in 1063.

A significant number of the moneyers' names on the coins of Aethelred II and his successors minted at Exeter and elsewhere in Devon were Scandinavian. Moneyers were the men who produced the coins on the king's behalf. Veronica Smart considers the number surprising for southern England. North and east of the Thames, in the later named Danelaw, where Scandinavians settled and were in control for some time, we would expect moneyers with Scandinavian names to appear. At York, for example by the end of the tenth century 75% of moneyers' personal names were of Scandinavian origin. For the reign of Aethelred II Exeter's moneyers included Cytel, Thurgod and Carla, while Wicing - a rare example of Vikingr as a personal name - was active in Lydford in Knut's reign. Under the latter king, Scula minted in Exeter and the name Farman appears on

Totnes coins a little later. But thereafter Scandinavian names disappear. In this same period Scandinavian names from mints south of the Thames are sparse. This group of names on Devon coins may suggest therefore that some families of Viking descent did settle in Devon; perhaps there was a small community in Exeter. We should however, bear in mind that these were specialists, who moved about - a moneyer named Wicing for example was minting in Worcester under Harold II - so this may not be proof of a settled community of Scandinavians in Exeter. Moreover, Domesday Book shows that Scandinavian names became popular even in well-to-do Anglo-Saxon families, so we cannot be certain that someone with a Viking personal name was necessarily of Scandinavian origin.

A number of pieces of late Saxon sculpture survive from Devon, mainly cross shafts. These include the pieces from Colyton, Exeter, Dolton, Chulmleigh and Sidbury as well as the Copplestone Cross, all identified and described by Masson Phillips. The Copplestone Cross was probably erected in about 905 to commemorate Bishop Putta who was murdered travelling in the area. It was certainly there by 974, when it is mentioned as a boundary stone in a charter. Its interlace patterns set in rectangular panels is reminiscent of similar decoration on other Devon pieces and on some of the Cornish crosses.

What is wholly missing from Devon however, are signs of the influence of Scandinavian art styles on stone sculpture.

This is in sharp contrast to Cornwall, where a number of crosses and memorials, distributed through the county, exhibit Anglo-Scandinavian styles. If these ideas were being brought to Cornwall by sea, as, for example, some sculptural motifs were transmitted along the north Welsh and Cumbrian coasts it is difficult to see why Devon missed out. The stronger influence on Devon may be from Wessex as, for example, the Colyton Cross suggests. Nevertheless the difference between Cornwall and Devon is not easy to explain in terms of chance survival and we may fall back on an idea, which has re-occurred through this account, that there were ties between the Cornish and the Vikings, even perhaps that there was a degree of Scandinavian settlement in Cornwall.

CONCLUSION

In conclusion, it should be asked: what effects did the Scandinavians have on Devon between 800 and 1069? Largely, it has to be admitted, the effects were indirect. Their actions caused an increase in the use of fortifications and thus the development of urban sites. The Devon landscape for the first time since the Roman period included towns. Moreover, systems were put in place to provide labour to repair, build and garrison these sites. The silver which the Vikings brought into the Irish Sea area and their own economic activities stimulated trade in the region and Devon participated in this from the late ninth century, when coins began to be minted at Exeter. Tenth-century pennies minted in Devon have been found in excavations in Dublin and contact with northern France is shown by French pottery from Exeter towards the end of that century.

Viking activities in the area may have delayed full control of Devon by the Wessex kings and the South West generally and knowledge of the British background of the territory perhaps encouraged Viking leaders to attack the peninsula and through it the West Saxon and English kings. Scandinavian settlement in Devon on any significant scale can hardly be claimed but along with the moneyers' names and the dedication of St Olave's church, it suggests that there was a Scandinavian element in Exeter's population before 1066. If so it was probably trading rather than raiding which brought them there.

FURTHER READING

J. Allan, C. Henderson and R. Higham, 'Saxon Exeter' in J. Haslam (ed.) *Anglo-Saxon Towns in Southern England* (1984), J. R. Maddicott, `Trade, industry and the wealth of King Alfred', *Past and Present* (1989, 123), 3-51, E. N. Masson Phillips, 'The ancient stone crosses of Devon Part II', *Report and Transactions of the Devonshire Association* (1938, 70), 299–340, D. M. Metcalf, 'The monetary economy of the Irish Sea province' in J. Graham-Campbell (ed.) *Viking Treasure from the North-West: The Cuerdale Hoard in its Context* (1992), 89-106 and P. Rainbird, 'Oldaport and the Anglo-Saxon defence of Devon', *Proc. Devon Archaeol. Soc.* (1998, 56), 153-164 were particularly useful in the writing of this book.

For general reading see J. Haslam, *Anglo-Saxon Towns in Southern England*, noted above, J. E. B. Gover, A. Mawer, and F. M. Stenton, *The Place-Names of Devon* (1931, 1932), i & ii, S. Keynes and M. Lapidge (trans.), *Alfred the Great, Asser's Life of Alfred and Other Contemporary Sources* (1983), P. H. Sawyer, *Anglo-Saxon Charters; An Annotated List and Bibliography* (1968) and M. J. Swanton, (trans. and ed.) *The Anglo-Saxon Chronicle* (1996) and B. Yorke, *Wessex in the Early Middle Ages* (1995).

Last Small Cross Penny. struck at Lydford.

Also available in the Concise Histories of Devon Series

Roman Devon	Malcolm Todd
Elizabethan Devon	Todd Gray
Devon and the Civil War	Mark Stoyle

Also by **The Mint Press**

The Devon Engraved Series

Exeter Engraved: The Secular City (2000)

Exeter Engraved: The Cathedral, Churches, Chapels and Priories (2001)

Devon Country Houses and Gardens Engraved (2001)

Dartmoor Engraved (2001)

The Travellers' Tales Series

Exeter (2000)

East Devon (2000)

Cornwall (2000)